Advance Praise

"Rod Carlos Rodriguez's *A History of Echoes: Poems* is brilliant Borínquen griot testimony told as only a poet of the highest order can tell it. While its essence is reminiscent of Latin mythmakers like Eduardo Galeano, and its free verse swaggers like early Victor Hernandez Cruz, its voice and rhythms and language are in a class of its own. In this impressive collection of historical Rican-struction, Rodriguez illuminates the poet's soul-quest for a home that no longer exists, and yet forever pulses in the blood. *A History of Echoes: Poems* is a powerful and timeless invocation, a resounding document of memory, 'a flashing heartbeat in twilight.'"
—Tim Z. Hernandez, author of *Some of the Light*

"In *A History of Echoes: Poems*, Texan poet Rod Carlos Rodríguez crafts a repository of the long marginalized, but not lost, cultural Taíno heritage. Poetry turns into an act of preserving the unique language, stories, and traditions of our Taíno ancestry. In this captivating and poignant collection of poems, and like a *bohíque* or shaman, Rodríguez's voice amplifies the polyvocality of presences that still stream down in our blood. His work pays homage to Taíno culture and its history with grace, depth, and beauty. *A History of Echoes* explores the complexities of identity, belonging, and memory as Rodríguez's poems sublimate into lyrical and evocative language, rendered with reverence and authenticity."
—Elidio La Torre Lagares, author of *Wonderful Wasteland and Other Natural Disasters: Poems*

"Rodriguez' exquisite lyricism sweeps through Puerto Rican history to the present. Each poem in *A History of Echoes* is a singular gem, but the expanse of this book immerses the reader deep into a mythic realm where music and rhythm take over, carry us on a profoundly sensuous journey. A gourd bursting open releases an ocean, sea turtles emerge from a wound in a man's back, ships arrive with 'ugly, / upright animals [who] seemed// as gods, at first,' men who speak 'ugly noise' and have 'buticaco eyes.' The horror of Spanish plunderers, visitations by gods to the contemporaries like the poet Julia de Burgos, and images of Puerto Rican freedom fighters seized my imagination and left me with awe for this book."

—Beverly Burch, judge & author of *Leave Me a Little Want*

Also By Rod Carlos Rodriguez

Published Poetry Collections

Exploits of a Sun Poet (as Rod C. Stryker)

Lucid Affairs (as Rod C. Stryker)

Native Instincts (as Rod C. Stryker)

Cantos, Incandescent

A History of Echoes

Poems

by Rod Carlos Rodriguez

Winner of the Gival Press Poetry Award

Gival Press

Arlington, Virginia

Published by Gival Press, an imprint of Gival Press, LLC.

For information please write:

Gival Press, LLC

P. O. Box 3812

Arlington, VA 22203

www.givalpress.com

First edition

ISBN: 978-1-940724-49-2

eISBN: 978-1-940724-50-8

Library of Congress Control Number: 2024945995

Cover art: © Cristina Crain

Design by Ken Schellenberg.

I dedicate this work to my wife, Sabina, whose clear vision and pure love I aspire to.

I also dedicate this work to the silent voices of Puerto Rico, past and present. I hope I have done them justice in my efforts to reclaim what was lost.

Finally, this work is dedicated to all of Puerto Rico's unsung martyrs and heroes who have fought and are still fighting
for freedom and independence.

Soy Antillano.

Contents

Rooting for Spices

Rooting for Spices

Caciques live
in my heartbeat,
swim in my corpuscles,
drown in my brown skin,
and are reborn
in my voice.

Their rushing rivers
part my curls,
pour through my
open iris
at 3am,
filter my vision
through mimosa leaves, golden sunsets,
Utuado mountains,
and the Adjuntas pueblo.

Taino paint my breath
in tongues
murmured down to
my toes, my hands,
the edges of my criollo.
Mi gente de
Mayagüez, Bayamon,
and Cabo Rojo
keep feeding, caressing
these roots
fatigued by
a half millennium
fighting güeros, Spanish Crowns,
and the Caribe.

I hear el piratas
whispering through
taste buds
embracing oregano,
cilantro, Sazón
and the body follows,
joins, leads me deep
into El Yunque's forest,
by diamond emerald
shores,
of Borike'n,
of home.

Xabao and the Cemi

It was the cemi's fault,
jumped
in her path,
shaped as obsidian
stone.

Being mere naborías, she knew
only
an elite nitaíno
or behique could
make sense of
it.

Jurakán's fast winds and gusts
paled
in speed and
agility to Xabao's
flight

across plateau, through forest, over
rocky
paths, she slid
into the village
behique's

ceremonial guaíza mask. Panting, head
lowered
in respect, Xabao
retold her run
in

with the obsidian cemi. Xiorro
was
meditating on the
village *areyto's* cohoba
laced

ceremony. He had little time
for
cemi, obsidian or
not. Too often
cemi

spirits were departed once Xiorro
arrived.
Xabao stood, staring
at her behique's
bare

and age-cracked feet. Soft
wind
streamed into their
silence. Xiorro relented,
spit

cohoba into the dirt, grabbed
his
daughter's hand and
ran to the
beach.

Xabao stopped. Knelt by obsidian
cemi,
Xiorro's eyes widened,
the spiritual force
of

the cemi pummeled his senses,
withered
any doubts, reverently
picked up his
daughter's

cemi, it spoke its dark
language
in his mind.
Presented its desired
shape

behind Xiorro's eyes, he cried
out,
fell to his knees,
Xabao knelt beside
him.

Held her father's shoulders, cemi's
dark
vision invaded her
mind as well.

Arrowhead,
for a would-be god named
Cristóbal de Sotomayor.

Xabao and Xiorro, terrified, prayed
cemi
might release them
from this heinous
path.

It brooked no denial.

The Jauca river
would receive
the Spaniard's blood.
Aguëbana II,

cacique to half of Borike,
would
commit the killing
shot. Xabao shook
her

head, her father cried and
forged
the obsidian arrowhead,
consigned to Borike's
doom.

Gente in Silence

What came before
Isabella-sanctioned genocide,

What came after
Atabey-lost to winds and

time.

No *areyto.*
Voices still.

Only artifact.

A smattering
of language.

What comes next
in shadows of

caciques and
postmemory.

Remember us.
Remember.

Salomé Waits

Beside Abacoa's river,
beneath Aruaca's
Cueva Ventana, she

caresses tobacco leaves,
gently presses them
between thumb and index finger.

Waits. As days, weeks,
decades coat the trail
back to his cave.

His promised kiss
remains moist on
her cohoba-laced lips.

Waits. Hours, months,
lifetimes season her belief
in Aruaca's return.

Even Yocahú rests
His hands on Salomé's
pale shoulders, whispers *patience*.

Waits. As coqui's cries serenade
behind last night's downpour.
Still angry at Don Julian's

rejection of Aruaca,
Salomé remains
unaware her lover

died at her father's
feet. She remains seated,
every night in Cueva Ventana.

Waits.

Creator's Curse

I

Scabs across my back,
chest, sores that
never heal. My brothers
suffer no affliction,
skin smooth
and honey brown,
true Gods in
our Celestial
lands of plenty.

Yaya's bohio
had many treasures,
I knew it was
forbidden.
My brothers cared
little.
I saw them
enter the bohio,
followed only
to scold them.

They wrestled for
the gourd hanging
from the ceiling,
I tried to catch it
as it fell,
burst on the floor,
an entire ocean
carried us away

from all we understood,
a new ocean world
of islands, rivers, and caves.

Still I
heard whispers of
our old home.
My brothers
thought I was mad,
they heard silence.
Separated, we explored
this water world,
sometimes my scabs
kept me weak.
But soon
I found a bohio,
Much like Yaya's.

My brothers were
there, waiting,
with an elder.
He said he was
our grandfather.
Bayamanacoa
extolled tales
of our lost mother,
Itibi Cahubaba,
over a meal of cassava.
We were grateful
for this knowledge.

II

Bayamanacoa kept staring
at my scabs and sores.

He inhaled
sacred medicine
through his nostril,
then flicked his nose,
potion flashed
on my back,
lightning pain
across my body,
arms spasmed,
vomit spewed
from mouth to floor.

My brothers, scared
at the sight, held
me, saw my back
swell, they flinched.
I felt the skin tighten,
expand, pain made
me cry out,
one of my brothers,
ax in hand,
cut me,
just between the
shoulder blades.
A beautiful sea turtle
emerged, crawled to
water's edge, swam and
populated our new world,
and I slept...many days.

Upon waking,
I still hear my
Celestial family,
glimpse their forms
sometimes at sunset,

sunrise. These gifts will pass
to those who follow
in my caracaracol footprints.

Hummingbird Blues

A pool of pure sky.
It's sapphire glow
lit Alida and Taroo's
faces,

she knew it was
wrong,
she knew
his touch burned.

Her father,
spittle rage-filled,
pushed her
into another's arms.

A coward's arms,
killing in thought
and action of
Taroo's tribe.

Her lover knew
her heart could
never beat to please
only her tribe.

She begged Atabey,
Yocahú, to save
her from her father,
this fate.

Her arms, her legs,

Flattened into red petals,
her eyes, her mouth
formed into stamens.

Taroo sits at their
pool, days, weeks,
cries and begs Atabey,
craves Alida's sweet fragrance.

His lips become
a needle-shaped beak,
arms form into
tiny wings,

he scents Alida's
bloom close to
the pool's edge,
flies to her flower,

they kiss once
more and always.

Struggle and Silence

1. The war is long,
Aracibo hikes
the hard, mountainous
trail to his yucayeque,
near Abacoa's banks.

2. Mabó...

3. Canóbana...

4. Hayuya...

5. Jumacao,
limping, wounds
fester in humid
twilight. No areyto
for many full moons,
but he learned
Spaniards are human.

6. Naguabo...

7. Güaraca...

8. Dagüao

9. In Turabo yucayeque,
Caguax orders
the entire village
put to the knife,
no slaves for

white demons,
like other caciques
have allowed.

10. Aramaná...

Columbus Day

Boricu'a saw the ships
with white cloths
as clouds, these

ships brought men
who spoke ugly
noise, like iguaca.

The ugly,
upright animals seemed
as gods, at first.

Some of us lacked
trust in their
shiny clothes

and their buticaco eyes.
They did not
honor the Bo'jike.

Then the cacique
tested one of
these gods, drowned

him. He stayed dead.
Now, Bohiti warns
of guazabara

as our bohios burn,
we make ready
to fight the evil

leaders they call Columbus,
Ponce.

Taino Language Key:

Boricu'a - The Valiant People of the Sacred House
iguaca - green parrot
buticaco - shifty eyes
Bo'jike - Great Lord of the Forest and Earth
cacike - Chief
Bohiti - shaman - a Taino spiritual leader
guazabara - war, warrior
bohios - roundhouses

Yahíma

She knew nothing
of empire, disease,

only warm nights,
feathers in
ebony strands
falling on
soft, brown shoulders.

She saw little
beyond her children,

faces painted,
dancing around fires
and bohíos.

She knew nothing
of conquest, greed,

only spirit lights
at twilight
trailing her hands
in luminous waves sliding,
whispering on beaches
by her yucayeque.

She saw little
beyond silence,

her parents murdered,
invaders weapons

painting blood
on anyone
protecting her
brothers and sisters,
Boricu'a, herself.

She saw nothing
the wind will ever reveal

after empire,
after greed,
after silence.

Magical Journeys and the New Puerto Rican

Juan's Fever

Gold: universal currency,
status, influence in palace,
trade councils, or Seville.

Growing up in the Kingdom of Leon
Juan knew
gold opened doors, consolidated
property, bought

just about anything anyone
could ever want or need.
These islands, these savages
must hide rivers of gold

Cristóbal Colón bragged of,
mountains of
precious metal, oceans glittering,
waiting, tempting.

Juan's avarice--prepared to
kill, rape, enslave,
drain any source, human,
animal, these Taíno surrounding

him, he marries the cacique's
daughter, ugly
face painted in indigo colors
and blood

red tones. Juan grudgingly
accepts the young woman's

brown, calloused hand as his
dreams flash in prized metal,

glinting in his new
wife's earlobes, then the fever
takes Juan's mind. A killing fever,

to consume all thought
save his yearning to live a long,
rich life, enjoy all the wealth,
he *will* kill, rape, enslave--multitudes.

In his gold-tinged hallucinations,
Juan Ponce
de Leon's captain whispers...a fountain, across
the waves...

Cristóbal

All of them,
or as many as possible,
must release their aberrant
lives to his blade.

One never opposed
Viceroy Colón.

Cristóbal de Mendoza
salved his conscience
by labeling them
cattle, herds to be
culled, for Spain,

for empire.

His gaze averted
as each man, woman,
child is slaughtered,
whole villages
silent except for the flies,
their low hum – rumbles
in warm sunsets,

for distant crowns.

His sleep measured
in small sips,
too many
blood-rimmed eyes
stare in silent

dreams, except for
the flies,

for gold and slaves.

Vieques, now empty of
villages, empty of all Taíno.
They live instead
in Cristóbal's nightmares.
Hundreds, thousands.
Like flies.

Like silence...

John White's 4th Voyage

Raleigh promised.
A fourth voyage, a Governorship,
John White wanted
a fresh start, a
new Virginia.

The fleet languished
in 1587,
an ugly little
island, some called
Beake, others
would name Vieques.

His men were hungry,
sheep ran wild,
standing water copious.
And twilight brought
witch-lit waves,
White reflected.

Twilight also brought
Her, a black-haired
woman, Her eyes
witch-lit as the waves,
an enchantress.
White asked
Her name. She answered
in his mind, *Atabey.*

Gibberish, he thought.
Then his men

started dying.
Was it the wild sheep?
The standing water?
Was it Her...
Atabey?

He and his men bolted
to their ships...
he ordered all speed
to his new Virginia,
away from
Beake, cursed islands,
Vieques,
away from Her.

Maboya and Cofresí

Four hundred souls,
with my own hands.
None were Puerto Rican.

Foreign frauds,
their gold
and laws and guns.

Two years of taking
their wealth, lives, ships.
The Catholics among

my crew pray
at our brazen, wanton
violations toward

our imperial masters.
Prayer is for
cattle sent to slaughter,

for puertorriqueños deprived
of what rightfully
belongs to them, to us,

to me. I have no time
for unjust gods
with deaf ears.

I'd just as soon pray
to the coqui and
his three toed feet.

Perhaps Yocahú
might pass my
treasures to mi gente

when Governor de la Torre
finally orders
my execution.

Four hundred lives,
snuffed out, with
these two hands.

Maboya and I parleyed,
out there on the waves,
a deal the God

swore would save
many lives, my wife,
my daughter.

We agreed who
should die.
The last one

Maboya will collect
owns my two hands.
Viva Puerto Rico.

-Captain Roberto Cofresí y Ramírez de Arellano, *El Pirata Cofresí* killed
300 to 400 people, mostly foreigners.

Diablo of San Cristobal

La garita
glows in preternatural
fire, flashes
and boils the waves
beating against
Castillo de San Cristobal,
cries of missing soldiers
echo across the hemorrhaging
bay and fade
in its depths.
Manuel, sick
to his stomach,
stands in the small
courtyard.

His turn to man
Garita del Diablo.
Mamá convinced
him to join
the Imperialist army.
She needed money
for comida y café.
He loves his Mamá.
More cries drift
in from the waves.
Manuel's feet
are sealed into
the flagstones,
his body, a cold
statue, waves
spraying his

granite countenance.

Barking from his
commanding officer,
safe and dry near
the castle walls
above, reanimates
Manuel, briefly.
Walks toward
the sentry box,
enters,
screams.

Guabancex, Her divine
anger satiated, picks
Her teeth with
Manuel's splintered
femur bone,
waits in Bahia
de San Juan.

Manuel's Mamá
still hears his cries
across the bay.

Campeche and the God of Storms

The commission from
the Spanish Crown
astonished José.

His reputation's reach
stunned even him
at times.

As always,
he collected
brushes and

paints from his
closet before
the knock

on his front door,
terrified when lightning
thunderously struck

at the same time, rain
started falling suddenly
on the roof.

The front door
opened, red eyes
bore into

Campeche's retinas, screeching
wind poured into
the house.

Grudgingly, he
allowed Jurakán into
his home.

Other paintings, completed
or not, were tossed about
the foyer,

José's 58-year-old
patience was at
an end.

He scowled at
the God of Storms and Lightning,
shushing Him.

Jurakán sat,
mortification resplendent across
His face.

Campeche quickly
grabbed rum and his sketch pad,
offered the drink

to his guest, waited.
Jurakán's screech
was stifled as

Campeche raised one
finger in
the air.

Quietly, said the host.
A small wind spilled

from divine

lips, *paint me*,
the wind said.
José's shocked

face flickered
briefly, calculating proper
angles and

dimensions of such
an amorphous figure,
this Jurakán.

José knew this
would be his most
glorious undertaking,

his fame would be
celebrated from Spain to the
Far East!

Even from the start,
painting Jurakán was
near impossible,

small cracks in the God's
smokey, churning skin
caused little bolts

of lightning to strike
walls, ceiling,
furniture, which caught

fire. Campeche was

forced to stop his work
just to

smother small flames or
clean up rain puddles
gathering in

his studio,
tiny downpours also
smeared his

paints every moment
he raised his paintbrush.
Campeche glared

at Jurakán, the artist's own
anger mounting, becoming
the embodiment

of his subject.
Finally, Campeche roared,
Stop fidgeting!

Instantly, rains ceased,
lightning--a ripple
of soft

glow in the background,
Campeche was able to
make progress

on his growing masterpiece.
A Madonna and Child, a San Juan Nepomuceno;
child's play

to this unruly,
uncontrollable icon of
the hurricane God's

image, taking
shape, Campeche's hand,
a blur

of activity and speed
the artist
never imaged

possible. Bent over,
Campeche gently mixed final
colors on

his palette, itself
a testament to the destruction
of Jurakán, Himself,

José Campeche y Jordán
leaned in, ready
to apply

the last brush stroke of
his master work
encompassing techniques

never to be fully embraced
for hundreds of years,
Jurakán briefly

glimpsed the portrait,
anger and rage
exploded in

the little studio.
José never had a chance.
All belongings,

paints, palettes, his other artwork,
finished or not, burned or
splintered into

a million, billion pieces,
then doused in a deluge,
spilling into

the street until neighbors
ran out of their
quiet homes,

frightened as Jurakán
screamed and ran
out of

José's now leveled
home. The God
kept screaming,

churning, raging,
leveling everything. None
were spared.

In time,
The God of Storms and Lightning moved on.
José's body,

discovered under the shattered
wreck of his house, was

still grasping

a small, torn corner
of his painting, a masterpiece
of El Jurakán.

Arroyo de Atabey

She spills
through building construction
and good intentions,
fills caracaracol pockets
with her waters,

sluices over
prescribed channels,
past crumbling monuments,
bubbles beneath lucid streams.

She drenches
pages and streets,
flooding words
through eyes,
over hearts.

She drives
under rain-slicked bridges,
a living river,
this arroyo de Atabey.

Jacinto, Dame la Vaca

Waves against rocks,
soft thunder
inside and beside
diamond-shaped void.

A fortnight, a month, half a year,
Jacinto and his cows visit
the beach, crystal blue
against the froth of white.
They never tire of

its solace, spray
of mermaid tears
blesses these treks.

Reina, vaca favorita,
kept her close, the rope
around both their waists,
an umbilical braided and taut,

a tightrope, an anchor, a safeguard?
Jacinto heard the raucous
boom of the wave, Reina's
screech, the back breaking
tug towards the well.

Jacinto yelled, Reina ran
faster, into the opening,
into churning, tumbling,
fading light, here by

Paseo Lineal Isabela,
here at Jacinto's Well.

Francisco, Betances, Spanish Crowns, and the Devil

after "El Velorio (The Wake)" by Francisco Oller

"They should all
look away, except
the old man, foreground,
mourns and weeps

a still born, every other eye
turned anywhere...except
his, arrested on the child's stillness,"

Oller decides. Mixes the oils,
drags the chair closer,
fights the seat cushions
for comfort. He paints

these Wake-attending
puertorriqueños,
inert and silent in their
morally offensive
celebrations.

But the old man,
reminiscent of Betances,
grieves the child
of a nation, left
to the devil's

jackals, ready to tear,
rend soft flesh and bone.

Betances' anguish
seeps from the
painting's oil, drips
and pools on every
gallery floor, every priest's
nave, every governor's marble
steps, stains diamond-encrusted

Spanish brows that never
wash clean.

Oller lays his brush
on his palette,
walks away.

La Brega and Reclamation

Julia De Burgos and Jurakán

Summers by the river's shore invite healing words in Julia's journal. Atabey whispers poems in Julia's ear of futures painted in poetry and sacrifice. She wakes to see a beautiful woman resting beside her, long dark hair flows around Her shoulders. *Hola, Abuela.* Julia commiserates the usual gestures of respect. Atabey exhales a small, slow smile. *Jurakán approaches.* The Goddess' words tickle, fill Julia's head. *Again, but He was here two weeks ago.* She hates Guabancex's son. Always angry and filled with killing winds. Julia, more respectful gestures given to the Goddess, walks to the river's edge. Gently splashes cool water on her face. *Warn mi gente, mi'ja.* Atabey is determined and testy today. *Of course, Abuela.* Julia gathers her journal and blanket, runs home as the clouds gather in rage and lightning.

Of her surviving brothers and sisters, only two believe Julia's warnings. Her parents are tired of Atabey's attachment to their oldest child. However, they know not to irritate the Goddess. *Gather your things, mi'jos! We have to run to the shelter, rapido!* Julia sees Atabey arguing with Jurakán by the neighbor's house. She and her family are running down the street, Jurakán's eyes glowing at them, His lightning, winds, and screams chase them toward the shelter in the village center. Just as they slam the heavy door closed, Julia briefly glimpses the wall of wind flattening houses and tossing cars. *Julia.* Atabey appears beside Julia, her parents scream in surprise. *My grandson will spare everyone if you will talk to him.* The Goddess' eyes are clear and shine in the shelter's low lighting. Julia kisses her parents' faces. *No Julia, Jurakán will take you from us!* Hugs her sisters and brothers. Quickly opens the door. It takes all her strength to close it.

Jurakán is screaming at Julia's back. She struggles to turn and face the God of thunder, wind, and lightning. Stares deep in His flashing eyes. Never wavers. *Enough, Jurakán!* Buffeting winds tearing at her body begin to slow. The stinging rain, crackling thunder, and lightning gently subside. Jurakán averts His gaze. Nods His head and walks over to the still standing Los Hijos de Borinquen bar. Grabs a beer. He begins arguing politics with Pedro Albízu Campos. Julia turns back, opens the door to the shelter. She and her family walk down the tree and bougainvillea littered road to rebuild what's left of their home. Julia's journal is right where she left it, Atabey still whispering in her ear.

Flora, Caciques, and Deminan

A small lookout post,
with red-orange stones,
built by Americanos,
invaders with no respect
of culture and tradition.
Flora watches
from the lookout's precipice,
her eyes flash to
the bay of Guánica,
settles on its splendor
fanning from
jagged hills to aquamarine
waves. First, Agüeybaná
then his brother, Güeybaná,
appear on either side.
Both caciques whisper in
a language Flora
doesn't understand,
one or two words float
as familiar resonance.
Her attention freezes
on Deminan's name.
Her adoptive family
had warned Flora
to never have
a child of visions:
a caracaracol.
Beside her,
Agüeybaná speaks
and Flora finally understands
his Borike'n words,

he will be born,
a child of the sun,
your grandson.

Flora flees down
El Fuerte Caprón's steps,
races down the rocky path
in her chanclas,
twice almost
twisting her ankle,
until she runs into the street.
She doesn't stop until
the doors of
San Antonio Abad Parraquia
loom above her.
Flora kneels on
the steps of
Guánica's famous church,
prays and gulps breaths,
fear and anxiety twitching
her eyes, her mouth,
continues begging
her Jesus for salvation,
pleads to be saved
from having a
caracaracol nieto.
Someone shakes Flora,
startled, wakes,
stares in confusion
at the priest,
the church entrance,
her knees aching from
kneeling on
stone steps.

Father Rodriguez speaks
in a language
she doesn't understand,
Agüeybaná's words
still echoing in
her head. The
cacique's portents
finally stop, and Flora
understands the priest's
words:

be not afraid,
my child,
your grandson
will lift up
many with his songs.

He gently guides
her into the church,
blesses her forehead
and joyfully praises
Flora's fortunate tidings,
a Deminan offspring
joining her family, soon.

Luis and Flora

A family calling.
Luis' father gave him
little choice.

A long line,
Rodriguez's of the
Lutheran cloth.

But his love
for Flora
echoed in

blood vessels
swimming in
his left and right

ventricles, in the
recessed membranes
of the amygdala,

in the Taino-
spark centered
between his eyes.

Flora begged him
to stop loving
her.

She remembered
the Caciques and
their vision.

Luis would never
stomach a caracarcol
in the holy lineage,

she could never
ruin this man
whose love

eclipsed her sight,
her fears,
her breath.

Flora revealed her
vision the afternoon
he decided

to kneel at
her feet, beg
her to be

his bride in
sight of God,
Jesus, and the angels.

A glimmer of
fear clouded Luis'
hazel eyes.

His arm remained
raised, refocused
his gaze on Flora's

deeply tanned face,
determined to purge

any such curse

of a caracaracol
from his offspring,
while Flora,

doubt hidden behind
her cherub face,
accepted Luis' proposal.

Xiorro and the Sun

Lost between
Bayamón roads
named Calle Angelina,
Calle 37,
once fields and
farms Xiorro worked
and bled, tilling
master's crops
before whispers
of freedom
for him, for his
brothers and sisters
in chains.

Now strange homes,
on strange streets
he drifts
as fog
rolling through
windows, gates,
front doors,
in Diana Resto's room,
her ears glisten
in Xiorro's whispers,
his anguish
settles in Diana's
pores, her blood,
a grief diffused
into DNA,
expelled through
Diana's children,

first Evelyn,
then Chinki,
Evelyn's Sheila,

onward to the
blond boy, sitting on
a hill, staring
at the sun, smiling,
Xiorro glinting in
this child's hazel eyes,
smiling in anguish,
moving in visions,
passed from abuela,
mama, niña,
to survive the monsters,
give Xiorro
and all who
ache release from
our prison,

to breathe,
to feel,
to heal,
to see
what
can be, should be,
will be

if only
to set Xiorro free.

Bodega Lights

Don Pedro counts the change,
eighteen dollars and ninety-eight cents,
gently lands the coins
in Elizam Escobar's
callused, paint-smeared hands.
Revolution red
bright on his right pinky.

In the corner, by the rack
of notebooks and ASPIRA
literary primers,
Oscar Jose Lopez avoids
thoughts like sedition,
conspiracy, but mulls over letters
like F and A, L and N.

Dylcia Pagán quickly
enters la Bodega, her mind
on the next cause that
MENDs her activism with
commitments towards country,
the people, struggle,
and independentista of soul.

Lolita Lebrón stands atop
the boxes of White Castle burgers,
screaming at shoppers,
her luger and voice drowned out
by the slurpy machine,
dripping on the feculent tiles
dingy with stars and stripes.

Holding Lolita's ankles,
Rafael Cancel Miranda
And Irvin Flores Rodríguez
glare at other customers,
chins out, even as
Andres Figueroa Cordero
waves a tattered, Puerto Rican flag.

Behind the counter,
Pedro Albizu Campos stops
counting change and fires
up the gathered nacionales,
a radioactive halo
surrounds him in holy
testament to martyrs
of Isla Del Encanto.

Lares de Oro

Mariana knits
in patches of blues and reds,
threads needles

through Betances' cry
for Lares, Utuado,
Adjuntas, and a Madrid

in flames.

Brazo de Oro
sews as if
possessed, she

sings in fields
of sacred sangre
beside Manuel and Miguel,

el gritos of tears.

A struggle that
pushes Yauco,
Rio Piedras, Ponce,

Belvis, Marti, Riojas,
Campos, Lebrón,
too many more,
crying, bleeding, dying

for visions drowned in

treaties and Guánica
invasions.
El grito remains

stillborn, cradled
in blood and bone
del Antillano

y Lares de oro.

A Jibaro's Son

Arrested for a flag.
A cloth of woven thread and colors bled
for independendista, for la gente.

.

Francisco's poor Jibaro papa, on the farm,
what would he say?
How would he see his son, sentenced

by oppressors and their dogs,
policia who worship
their Americano federales?

In prison, Matos' breakdowns
herald Atabey's
presence, solitary cell

blinded by Her radiance.
She begs him,
No cantes a lo locura.

But still, he sings,
still he breathes dark
fugues in spasms

wrapped around a flag,
a few threads colored
in familia, la gente,

para Puerto Rico.

Footnote to a Jibaro's Son

Francisco Matos Paoli,
a Puerto Rican poet,
arrested in 1950,
sentenced to 30 years
in prison. His *crimes*:

displaying a Puerto Rican
flag, giving four speeches
in support of Puerto Rican Independence.

Subsequently, a nervous
breakdown from prolonged
periods of solitary confinement
at La Princesa prison
in San Juan, Puerto Rico.

After his unconditional pardon,
he wrote *Canto a la locura,*
inspired by his experiences
in prison.

Words, Words, and Cantos

after "Words Words" by Iris M. Zavala,
translated by Roberto Marquez

Cantos, cantos
sung to diseased politicians
with oil-black irises
shaped in bullion,
American flags
draped on
mustangs crashing
in Ponce, San Juan,
it's 2021,
long dead
sugar factories,
naval kill zones
in Vieques,
earthquakes and Jurakán
crush Humacao,
Fajardo, and Caguas.
The drums,
Covid silent,
puertoriqueños in misery
vomit their hate
of politicians or
flags,
streets flooded
with regurgitated
breakfasts and café con leche,
where la colonia
seethes and bleeds,

mas cantos, we beg.
We sing.
Sing.

Ponce, Murdered

Such a pretty day, "La Borinqueña" playing in the streets, March 21st, 1937. *

Men in fine suits,
Women in pretty dresses,

The flags were big and proud and flying for Puerto Rico, for independence.

So many of us
marching, smiling.

Ponce, welcoming us and our cause with open arms, we embraced all

our sisters and brothers,
a shared struggle.

The church bells rang, my brother Miguel fell in the street, blood pouring

from his mouth,
he was trying

to speak, to breathe, others started falling and running, that's when I heard

gunfire, smoke,
screams, my arm,

like fire exploded inside and I ran, holding the gaping wound, crying and
yelling,

they chased us,
la policia, their

rifles pointing at us, people around me dying, running, pleading for them to

stop, please no more—

I stumbled, my leg was bleeding, my hair in my face. I waited, policia ran past,

held my breath,
closed my eyes

I heard the sobs, the cries of men, women, children. All of them, bleeding,

Miguel, my friends,
Ponce, sweet Ponce,
murdered.

*On March 21st, 1937, 21 people were massacred and 200 were wounded by the Puerto Rican Insular Police. They were ordered to commit this heinous crime by the then appointed governor of Puerto Rico, General Blanton C. Winship. The march in Ponce was a celebration for the end of slavery in Puerto Rico and a protest for the wrongful arrest and conviction of Pedro Albizu Campos, leader of the Puerto Rican Nationalist Party.

Places and Dominance

Streets among wooded
paths, towns with names
like Bayshore, Brentwood,
Lake Ronkonkoma.

Roam and assimilate,
languages other than
English, discouraged,
battered for skin-color,

heritage, dirty Puerto Rican,
running, escaping,
hating a history
never taught, severed
traditions to

hide from white teachers,
neighbors, police
who demand inculcation
of their dominance,

running, racing,
berating ghosts
drawn from Bayamon,
San Juan, Cabo Rojo

and a fight lost
before inception,
deceptive and comfortable
in my colonized mind

built of playing
cards, beatings, and
scars buried to
my marrow.

A fight--unremembering
their parental
belief in pleasing
white mindsets

in places named
Ponce, Utuado,
Rincon, and Borike.

Recipe for Illumination

Sixteen prayer ties:
cotton squares,
all in red.

A pinch of
tobacco and sage
in each square,

folded, tied into
little pouches,
strung together.

The string must
be red cotton, too.
Concentrate,

focus on key
questions as these
little pouches

form. Store in
a high place until
the Sweat Lodge.

Fast Twenty-four hours
before ceremony.
Maybe just herbal tea.

Day of Sweat Lodge,
strip down,
only shorts

and cold morning
air, enter Lodge.
Sweat. Sweat.

First person drones
about their question,
lightning bolt

shoved into
top of the skull,
Deminan's vision blinds,

body vibrates,
a live wire
in every nerve,

every blood vessel,
you are everything,
everyone! Sweat.

Excuse yourself,
exit Sweat Lodge.
Let bake in

bright afternoon
sun.
Reborn.

The Stare

He stares
up through his eyebrows
at the photographer,
a shy grimace
of the moment
etches the lips,

a pink, damp towel
his only shield
against a present,
a future of abuse,

neglect. My brother
also faces the camera,
head down,
wrapped in Diana's
half embrace,
eyeing an equal future
that will twist him,
form callouses on
his anger and hate.
Rosie, Laura, Elsie
surround us,

a pretense of shelter
in summer bliss,
flashes of fun,
few and futile.

I want to
climb into

that summer photograph,

hold my
four-year-old self,
impossibly brace
him (us) for what's to come.

Face our father as
I am now,
for both of us.

Still he stares,
as if promising me
we'll make it
through the
abuser's rage,
eventually,
for both of us.

Blanquito and the Sun

after *Vita Nova* by Louise Glück

She dreamed me, I still remember it.

A glimmer of fear; her old eyes swimming in prescience.
Whispered, since the void is empty with silence.

Then she hurried, past the Catholic sin of her third eye.

She spoke of a meadow, rolling hills, and an infant,
a smile and blonde hair, green eyes laughing at the sun,
in perfumed breezes, he sat.

Blanquito. That one is special,
her hands shaking and pointing at his rose-colored cheeks,
and laughter on that hill, a true eye thrown to a future;
perchance riddled with beatings, and rejection.

Cruel
blessings and Hail Marys
blacken Great-Grandma's vision

of me, a spite buried years ago.

Shining as a witness, my sun
holds me safe within Muses and faith—

though steeped, her prophecy,
untouched by age,
realized by Connecticut summers,

strung together
in Beat voices and
3am movements,
ravenous for art and love and light—

And this dream, those green eyes, now hazel
smiling on bright rolling hills.

Her third eye turned that key, rhyme
and verse and visions of poets
under a warm sun, a smiling star.

Mal Oro

Their eyes are
butcher knives,
engulf as raging fire,

orbs of drowning pool blue,
oily shale brown,
shady mixed hazel,
duplicitous green.

A natural human
habit-to gaze

into the eyes,
into the hate,
buffeted by
gelatinous fear
of my olive-skinned face,

my livid face,
my Latino state

of being, bleeding,
seeing, heeding, needing,
reeling from
efforts to make me
their criollo other. Create

me as another
stock figure, foreign

sinner for walking,

breathing, fucking,
peeing, crying,
kneeling before
their cross of burden,

their loss of certainty-
in my brown eyes.

Always the eyes,
always.

Pots and Pans and Reggaeton

The ghosts whisper *¡Que Mierda!* in his ear as pots and pans bang over and over in front of La Fortaleza. Reggaeton blasts the walls down. Governor Ricardo Rosselló sits in his office, hears those damned pots drilling into his brain. He wishes he'd never sent those Telegram texts. Fantasmas in La Fortaleza laugh at him, his weakness a cause of great derision and scorn. And the pots and pans won't stop, hundreds of thousands, a million pairs of hands pound his temples, demand his resignation.

His father, Pedro, hates reggaeton. Criminalized it. It just kept getting stronger, a chameleon on steroids.

Ricardo hates Telegram. But he can't criminalize it, since he used it so much, cursing miscreants and mayors. He stares at the resignation letter on his desk in front of him.

The pots and pans are getting louder. Old San Juan is flooded with screaming Puerto Ricans.
La Fortaleza is under siege. Banging, banging...and banging. Reggaeton blaring. The ghosts are still laughing, now in front of his desk. Ricardo scowls at their taunts and curses. He decides he too hates reggaeton and picks up the pen.

Playa Sucia in Twilight

One of these days a speaker's words will drone on just before the peppy strumming of Thomas Jefferson Wild's "I've No More Fucks to Give" blares out of nowhere, invading the quiet tears of friends and family, more friends than family. Nervous, anxious laughter will erupt from one or two, maybe Will or Sarah, necks craning to find out who started the song. The gathered, grieving expressions will focus on a woman, red-rimmed eyes smiling at everyone, defiant and pleased. Her hand will rest on the urn, etched with filigree shaped in a manifesto and a Muse's whisper, placed between the pernil, the white rice, red kidney beans, this poem, and a plane ticket tucked in her long jacket--San Juan, Puerto Rico stamped on the front.

Another one of these days a boat will stop, close to Playa Sucia, Cabo Rojo Lighthouse flashing on the coast. The waves will gurgle and lap the boat, almost upending the urn, etched with liminal shadows that slip between these words, forcing her to clutch at it. Not quite ready. She'll listen for that Spring in 2011, effortlessly floating on her back, closer to Sucia's beach. I had been playing with the new underwater camera, taking snaps of her, of us, of the warm water we never wanted to leave. She'll wait to hear that one photo I took of her, gazing toward the beach's slow crescent, curving in the distance. Then, she'll empty my ashes into waters my DNA came from, gaze once more at the lighthouse, a flashing heartbeat in twilight.

Suma

A smattering of cemis, artifacts, and genocide in Borike'n, Vieques, Culebra,
where coqui's cries serenade Salomé every night as Deminan's scabs

    and scars burn and blister--gifts for us all. Taroo's
    lover begs for
    needle beaked kisses beside pools and seas filled
    with luminescence

        and kin, blessed with Atabey's smile,
        Her holy gaze turned away from
        Aracibo and Caguax, Jumacao, and all
        caciques the Spaniards have

    slaughtered, bohios razed to the ground for a
    Cristóbal Colón, a Ponce
    de Leon, and we're left with Yahima's silence,
    fountains, and gold,

flies humming over villages, quiet and still, no Atabey to scare away
a John White, no Cofresí to wage a one-man war against imperialists,

    foreigners, or Governor de la Torre. Guabancex
    laughs at Spanish
    soldiers, Her son, Jurakán, tosses a painter's
    house, an island colony,

        no mercy, just crumbling buildings and
        hearts gliding down arroyos
        of Atabey. Jacinto's Reina bellows in
        wells and cruel Caribbean surfs

thundering over Wakes and a nation Betances
mourns for, pleads for
Oller to dream independence in Julia Burgos'
journal as she struggles

with spoiled Gods laying waste to countryside and coast, while an author's
abuela fights against cacique spirits and caracaracol portents, since
mournful

are the cries of Xiorro, his spirit is restless for
justice and broken chains,
before a broken Don Pedro and an angry Lolita
fight White Castle shoppers

and dingy tiles painted in stars and stripes.
But Mariana still threads her
needle for flags and still-born visions
made of blood, bone, and Antillanos.

So how is displaying a cloth of hope, a flag of
promise by a jibaro's son
tantamount to prison and solitary visits from
Atabey? What Covid silent words

are seething and bleeding cantos of illicit misery and mas colonia drums
for a dying Ponce, screaming and running, sobbing and praying

for no more massacres? And New York streets
force a forgetting of heritage, Cabo
Rojo, beatings, and marrows filled with Utuado,
Borike. Now, illumination

in cosmic Lodges reawakens holy
connections, pumps blood

vessels to contend with festering wounds
from abusive fathers, remembering

abuela visions of sun-drenched hills and rosy
cheeks beneath green
eyes and smiling stars. This Creóle other, Latino
sinner eyes a future

with pots, pans, and fantasmas forcing change en Isla del Encanto waiting
for that day in twilight on crescent playas by a flashing lighthouse where

I return to origins and the sea. Because this is
how I root out spices,
from DNA to 3am visions, from Taino breath to
whispering piratas,

in Sazon, cilantro, oregano, and rain
forest tongues. I am home.

Acknowledgements

"Columbus Day", has appeared in my previous poetry collection, *Native Instincts*, under my former pen name, Rod Carlos Stryker.

"Rooting for Spices," "Salomé Waits," and "Bodega Lights" have been published in the Contemporary Surrealist and Magical Realist Poetry anthology, published by Lamar University Literary Press (Jonas Zdeny, Editor), December 2022.

About the Author

Rod Carlos Rodriguez has an MFA degree in Creative Writing from the University of Texas at El Paso and is a Lecturer at the University of Texas at San Antonio Writing Program. He is a poet, fiction, and non-fiction writer who has been writing for over 40 years. He has four books of poetry published: *Exploits of a Sun Poet* (Pecan Grove Press, 2003), *Lucid Affairs* (Sun Arts Press, 2012), *Native Instincts* (Human Error Publishing, 2016), and *Cantos, Incandescent* (Finishing Line Press, March 2024). He is founder/chair of the Sun Poet's Society, South Texas's longest running weekly open-mic poetry reading (1995-2022). He has been nominated for the San Antonio Poet Laureate in 2012, 2014, 2016, and 2018. He was poetry editor for *Ocotillo Review*, a literary journal/periodical and he was the editor of the *Texas Poetry Calendar 2023* (Kallisto Gaia Press).

Photo by Sabina de Vries.

Poetry from Gival Press

Abandoned Earth by Linwood D. Rumney

Adama: Poème / Adama: Poem by Céline Zins with English translation by Peter Schulman

A History of Echoes: Poems by Rod Carlos Rodríguez

Architects of the Imaginary / Los arquitectos de lo imaginario by Marta López-Luaces with English translation by G. J. Racz

Arlington Poets in Solidarity with Ukraine edited by Robert L. Giron

Bones Washed in Wine: Flint Shards from Sussex and Bliss by Jeff Mann

Box of Blue Horses by Lisa Graley

Canciones para una sola cuerda / Songs for a Single String by Jesús Gardea with English translation by Robert L. Giron

Dervish by Gerard Wozek

Disputed Site: poems by Kate Monaghan

The Great Canopy by Paula Goldman

Grip by Yvette Neisser Moreno

Haint by Teri Ellen Cross Davis

Honey by Richard Carr

Let Orpheus Take Your Hand by George Klawitter

The Silent Art by Clifford Bernier

Some Wonder by Eric Nelson

Songs for the Spirit by Robert L. Giron

Songs for the Spirit / Canciones para el espíritu by Robert L. Giron with
    Spanish translation by Javier Prieto Martínez

Tickets for a Closing Play by Janet I. Buck

Twelve: Sonnets for the Zodiac by John Gosslee

Voyeur by Rich Murphy

We Deserve the Gods We Ask For by Seth Brady Tucker

Where a Poet Ought Not / Où c'qui faut pas by G. Tod Slone

For a complete list of Gival Press titles, visit: www.givalpress.com.
Books available from Ingram, Brodart, Follett, your favorite bookstore,
on-line booksellers, or directly from Gival Press.

Gival Press, LLC
PO Box 3812
Arlington, VA 22203
givalpress@yahoo.com
703.351.007

www.ingramcontent.com/pod-product-compliance
Lightning Source LLC
Chambersburg PA
CBHW020211090426
42734CB00008B/1016